For the most important job we will ever have.

Ron Campbell

SITUATIONAL PARENTING®

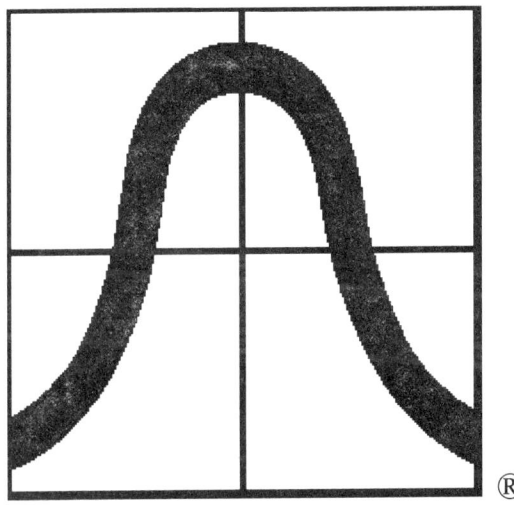

Dr. Paul Hersey
Ron Campbell
The Center for Leadership Studies

CLS

Situational Parenting is published by:

Center for Leadership Studies
230 W. Third Ave.
Escondido, CA 92025-4180

Copyright © 1999 Center for Leadership Studies
All rights reserved.

Printed in United States of America
Published, Escondido, CA
Center for Leadership Studies, © 1999

10 9 8 7 6 5 4 3 2 1

Library of Congress Cataloging in Publication Data

Hersey, Paul and Campbell, Ron
    Situational Parenting

1. Title.

ISBN 0-931619-03-3

(Family & Relationships)

To the Ones We Love
Suzanne Hersey
Dorothy Campbell
and our children and grandchildren.

A special thank you to Leslie O'Brien for the terrific
editing job and getting pushey on deadlines.
To Diane "Eagle Eye" Schmitz, mispelling, tense changes,
independent clauses, and dangeling participals -
thank you for your special gift.
And Mike Barksdale who accommodated,
to many "one last changes".

Our sincere appreciation to clients and
friends who have been very giving of
encouragement for this book.

Dear Reader,

If we could get to know each other you would soon discover that I am not one to procrastinate. It would be fair to say that I could be rightly accused of prematurely jumping into action. Yet I have engaged in every creative means imaginable to avoid finishing this book. There are, of course, good reasons.

First, how can anyone possibly believe they can write a book that does more than scratch the surface of something so complex as parenting? Answer, you can't! You simply cannot put all of life's lessons in a book. We can, and will, share with you some of our experiences plus those shared by many dedicated parents we met during this effort.

Second, this book is a rewrite of a labor of love, first accepted and responded to by Dr. Paul Hersey and Ken Blanchard in 1978. Paul had been after me to get this project moving for several years. Something in me couldn't get excited about collaborating or editing old "stuff." I believe our own relationship had to mature. For many years Paul has been my boss, eventually he became my mentor. To use a metaphor of his (borrowed from Sir Isaac Newton), "if I can see farther than others, it is because I have stood on the shoulders of giants." Paul is a giant, in his understanding of human behavior, in the field of behavioral sciences and as a friend impacting the lives of those close to him.

Our relationship has taken another step that was awkward for me and difficult to explain. Recently while reading a book on Native American culture I discovered a term that most aptly describes Paul in our present relationship – father friend. I don't think that at forty plus years I was looking for a father, perhaps that is why I found one. To Paul, thank you for one of the most rewarding and personal bonds of my life. I am honored.

Third, this writing is tough. Not the intellectual part or material content. What is hard is embracing the learning from life's lessons. Behind every piece of content in this book that suggests a certain course of action there lays numerous mistakes, some deep regrets and tons of forgiveness from loved ones (spouses and children).

I really wish you could receive these pages of information and examples as they were developed – sitting in the office with Paul, next to the fireplace, over a cup of coffee drinking wisdom from one of the best storytellers that ever lived.

Join us,
Ron

Introduction

Our ten-year-old neighbor, A.J., was sitting glumly on his front steps; chin in hands, looking very bored.

"Hey, A.J.! What's the matter?" We called over.

"There's nothing to do," he answered. "There's no Little League practice today. The playground is closed. And my parents won't let me go to the video arcade alone."

A.J.'s dilemma started us thinking. Were we ever bored as kids? We couldn't remember many times – there always seemed to be something to do. Why the difference? Why do many young people today seem so apathetic at school, at home and even at play? Why the increasing number of successful or attempted suicides at early ages? How can things like drugs, gangs and living on the streets become real options to our youth?

Looking for ways to explain the difference, we noted that as kids we had no one to blame for our boredom but ourselves. We played baseball without Little League. There were no playground directors. The responsibility for entertaining ourselves was ours and ours alone. If we wanted to play baseball, we first had to find a place to play. This generally meant getting together a group of neighborhood kids to scout out a vacant lot, get permission from the owner to use it and then begin the job of clearing off the rocks and raking the field.

We had no coaches, uniforms or fancy equipment. In fact, for years we thought a baseball was black rather than white because we'd never seen one that wasn't held together by tape. And one thing that guaranteed a spot on the team was to own a bat. If one broke, we hammered nails into it for support to keep it together. When it came to learning the skills of the game we were on our own. We picked up information from the "big kids" and taught it to each other.

And when we felt cocky enough, we'd challenge a similar group of kids a few blocks away. And before long we'd challenge another group a few blocks further away. Pretty soon we had a "little league" of our own, going strong.

Who did the planning? The organizing? The motivating? The kids did.

Who does these things today? The little league director. The coaches. The parents. In fact, anyone but the kids. All they have to do is show up for practice and games. They have beautiful fields, uniforms and even refreshment stands complete with parents working the booths.

And even if they have better skills than earlier generations, haven't today's kids lost something even more important? Have adults taken away their opportunities for leadership, creativity, responsibility and learning to constructively fill free time? Have we deprived them of the chance to experience and deal with life?

We know that today, parenting is a tougher, more demanding job than ever before. The obstacles seem more numerous and the stakes seem higher. Many children live in single-parent families where the entire burden of parenting falls on one adult (who probably works a full-time job). Even in two-parent families, nearly seventy percent of today's households have two working parents. Parenting is a full-time job and, even though we have a limited amount of minutes for influencing our children, our effectiveness depends on how we use those very special minutes.

It sometimes requires more love to stand back and let our kids "go it on their own," than to guide their every move.

But like the lessons learned on those gray and dusty ball fields long ago, we know that the frustrations, anxieties, triumphs and rewards experienced as kids are a necessary part of growing up. There is no way we can have those "experiences" for them. We can only be there for them, as parents.

Table of Contents

CHAPTER 1 *Dare to Care* 7

CHAPTER 2 *Influence* 15

CHAPTER 3 *Readiness* 29

CHAPTER 4 *The Model* 55

CHAPTER 5 *Building Success and Self Esteem* 77

CHAPTER 6 *Discipline - vs - Punishment* 87

CHAPTER 7 *Because I said so* 103

Parent Role Defined - for the purpose of this book we extend the role of parent to those adults engaging in a significant influence role in the family life of a child. We do not think of parent as a biological function. A parent conceives a child in the heart and delivers the child with love, compassion, and guidance.

A hundred years from now ...
It will not matter what my bank account was,
the sort of house I lived in, or the kind of car I drove.
The world will be different because
I was important in the life of a child.

Chapter One
Dare to Care

This book is about Situational Parenting where caring and learning to demonstrate care will have a significant impact on our children here, now and far into their adulthood. Success and effectiveness in parenting is determined by what we do in the here and now intertwined with the numerous lessons we need to live our lives as happy, healthy, responsible contributing members of society. Throughout all of this, it is important to remember that we, as parents, are not perfect and neither are our children. Mistakes will be made, words will be spoken and forgiveness comes in realizing that "I am loved," and acceptance can be just one communication away.

In our other life, at the Center for Leadership Studies, we have for decades provided leadership, sales and customer service training programs for organizations around the world. Regardless of which program we conduct, the information we share or the skills we work to develop, our efforts are merely intellectual exercises if the person doesn't *care*.

However, caring does not guarantee success; not caring does ensure failure!

As parents, we accept as fact that we do indeed care. The tricky part comes when *demonstrating* the care in both the tender moments and during tough times. By tough times we are referring to learning not to bite other children, not to hit the dog, picking up their toys, etc., and you can age the examples to match the growing child. By demonstrating care we mean addressing the issue without the dramatics of anger, punishment and most importantly, ignoring the apathy displayed by inappropriate behavior.

Adding another dimension, each attempt we make to influence our children simultaneously impacts them on two scales — success and effectiveness.

Success — having the desired impact on behavior
and
Effectiveness — maintaining a healthy cooperative attitude

How simple it would be if our goal was just to be successful and effective. Instead we need to make choices, at times accomplishing success at the expense of effectiveness and/or the other way around. On many occasions, we have all insisted that a higher level of success must be achieved at the cost of immediate cooperative attitude. Take as an example the four-year-old needing to obey the rule of not riding his new "hot wheels" in the street. Regardless of the other kids riding theirs, and the temptation of the street appearing to be a great place to ride. Whether they like it or not, regardless of how much they want to ride in the street, it is not allowed.

There are moments in the daily lives of all parents when we feel great about a nice try or a good intention on the child's part, even when the success just isn't there. Think back to the lovingly prepared lunch when you were served the sandwich of torn up bread from the awkward spreading of peanut butter. It was certainly more important to appreciate the act of kindness than remark about aesthetics. Some of the proudest moments as parents come from witnessing our children overcome fear or apprehension and giving something a try, regardless of how successful the outcome.

A real threat to Effective Parenting is apathy and/or a fear of failure. Apathy by definition is appearing to have a lack of interest or concern. To the child it means you don't care. They don't see over worked, busy or trying to build a better life for them. They don't see it as tired at the end of a long workday or spread too thin. To the child, there is simply an unfulfilled need for your involvement in their life. How do we fail with our children?

By being too intrusive or too removed
Too strict or too lax
Being cautious or being reactive
Trusting them or not trusting them
Treating them like children or pushing them to be adults
Teaching them winning is everything or trying is good enough
And the beat of life's contradictions goes on and on.

We, one and all, will have small failures at one time or another. The good news is that our children will survive as long as we deliver a consistent message that we care. Given the premise that we do care, the big question is *how do we show it* and do we show it in a way that is perceived and accepted by the child?

We trust that we can improve on the hope that someday, at some point in our children's adult lives they will look back and understand that they were loved. There is simply too much at stake to leave this message of being loved up to chance.

How do we show it?

- First, the expectation is not "everyday in every way." Children handle exceptions, off moments, and even off days if they are not too frequent. The question to ask yourself is; is enough love demonstrated to establish that being loved is normal? Is the prevalent feeling the child experiences one of caring or one apathy?

- Exactly when do we show it? The type and timing of attention is critical. Again, we are not striving for perfection. What is normal about the parents' behavior is that this is the way the child thinks of them - warm, cold, encouraging or distant?

- At the risk of making a dangerous understatement, there are four general types of reinforcement. **Positive** – "You did a great job on that picture" or "That was so nice of you"; **Negative** – "Sit down and stop acting like an idiot" or "Let me finish it, you'll screw it up"; **Conditional** – "I would be proud of you if" or "If you really loved me you would"; and lastly **Extinction**. Extinction is where the child is not acknowledged. No one cares enough to praise or punish. A childs strong need for reinforcement is to such a degree that faced with feelings of extinction they may choose to suffer negative reinforcement. This is particularly true when experience tells them that the probability of getting positive reinforcement is nonexiste. In other words, negative strokes are better than no strokes at all. Consider the two-year-old child stuck in a room full of adults. After several unsuccessful attempts to be acknowledged the child looks Mom or Dad directly in the eye and pours their drink on the carpet. Now the child will get some attention.

Why don't we show it?

Well, the problem is not with the child. Or at least it didn't start that way. So let's stop talking about the children for a moment and focus on the parents. If things are or have been so bad that we are truly unable to express love, we need to seek professional help. Seriously, you know the torment well enough not to want to inflict it on others. There is a large enough population lacking sufficient role models for appropriate behavior thereby hindering them from becoming comfortable with expressing love. Here are two great pieces of news for this population. One, we each get two lives, one we are born with and the other we make. And each day we get to write another part in our own legend. This couples nicely with the second piece of good news. Each child comes to you a unique clean slate. They don't judge the love you show them, they absorb it. They have no ulterior motives and suspect none from you. Children are, without a doubt, the safest people in the world to love and to be loved by. To a child, it is not what they have in their lives that matters, but *who* they have in their lives.

The following poem, "Children Learn What They Live," written by Dorothy Nolte succinctly captures volumes of information on child rearing. Take a moment to give yourself an extra treat by reading it slowly a second time.

Children Learn What They Live

If children live with criticism,
They learn to condemn.
If children live with hostility,
They learn to fight.
If children live with ridicule,
They learn to be shy.
If children live with shame,
They learn to feel guilty.
If children live with encouragement,
They learn confidence.
If children live with tolerance,
They learn to be patient.
If children live with praise,
They learn to appreciate.
If children live with acceptance,
They learn to love.
If children live with approval,
They learn to like themselves.
If children live with honesty,
They learn truthfulness.
If children live with security,
They learn to have faith in themselves and others.
If children live with friendliness,
They learn the world is a nice place in which to live.

Copyright © 1972/1975 by Dorothy Law Nolte, Ph.D.

Choose your words carefully,
They have more impact than you will ever know.
As a parent, you will discover
That it only takes a few seconds to open profound wounds
Or - with thought – help and heal.

Chapter Two
Influence

Join us as we explore two observations recently shared with us. The first, that as a parent we could not recall one hurtful comment, not a single attacking statement that we made on purpose. Second, nearly all parenting moments (when we are talking with our children) are reactive. All too much of our behavior is *not* on purpose…

The Crowleys were getting ready to take their seven-year-old son Andrew to his grandparents' fiftieth anniversary dinner. This wasn't a prescription for disaster as Andrew had well-developed social skills for a seven-year-old. Now thirty minutes before departing, Andrew understood the meaning of "a dress-up affair."

"You mean I have to wear a tie?" Andrew moaned.

"Yes," his mother said. "Now go get dressed or we'll be late."

"But I don't know how to tie it," Andrew mumbled, looking at his shoes.

"Of course you do," his father replied. "I showed you how to do it last week, remember? Now move along, Andrew, we need to leave soon."

Twenty minutes later, his parents calling impatiently from downstairs, Andrew reappeared. His red tie was hopelessly knotted on one side of his neck in a series of knots neither parent had ever seen before. As his father struggled to undo Andrew's handiwork he looked at his watch and growled, "Now we are really going to be late. I showed you how to do this last week. Can't you remember anything?" Andrew started to cry.

Of course, at tense moments like this we are all at our parenting best (worst). Andrew didn't know how to tie his necktie and no amount of pressure from his parents could suddenly give him that ability. What Andrew needed, and didn't receive from his parents, was the guidance that would have enabled him to do what his parents were asking of him.

or

Thirteen-year-old Sally has been mowing the lawn since early spring and she's very good at it. She likes running the lawn mower and seeing the finished results of her work, plus earning a few extra dollars to spend as she pleases. Dad's a member of the Air National Guard and he's been traveling every weekend to qualify as a crew member in a new airplane. For a change, he's home this weekend and he's trying to slide back into family life. As Sally brings out the mower he seizes the opportunity to get involved. He starts by explaining how to properly start the lawn mower and progresses to a lecture on safety procedures. He's telling her to start mowing near the house and to mow in a cross-pattern from the driveway to the sidewalk.

As Sally mentally drifts off, he demonstrates the proper technique by mowing a few rows, all the while asking her whether she understands what he's showing her.

"Of course I understand, Dad," Sally replies with some impatience. "I've been doing it all by myself for the last two months."

Dad can't understand Sally's snappy response. Shrugging his shoulders, he retreats dejected into the house.

Guidance and Support

In neither situation did the parent intend to be hurtful. Unfortunately it is our behavior — or how we act — that has more impact than our intentions. The two situations previously described illustrate the need for different types of Parenting Behavior. With the wisdom of twenty-twenty hindsight, we can see that Andrew really did not know how to tie his own tie, even though he had been shown how to do it before. Andrew needed guidance in how to perform the task his parents were asking of him. He needed, in fact, step-by-step directions, hands-on assistance and instruction in performing the task.

In Sally's situation, she clearly possessed the knowledge needed to operate the lawn mower. What she needed from her father was a little support and reinforcement rather than the close direction she received. She needed "stroking" and a show of appreciation for her willingness and ability to do the job.

Most Parenting Behaviors can be divided into two distinct categories:

Directive Behavior and Supportive Behavior

Directive Behavior involves one-way communication. We call it **guidance**. Andrew's parents needed to show him exactly how to tie his necktie; step-by-step. Directive Behavior is determined by the *extent* the parent provides the who, what, when, where and how that something is to be done.

Supportive Behavior involves two-way communication. It is the *extent* we engage in actively listening, praising, reinforcing and encouraging the child's ideas and suggestions. We call it **support**. Sally's Dad needed to listen to her, provide recognition and praise for her abilities, and give her a little positive reinforcement for her willingness and ability to tackle the front lawn.

Parenting Behavior tends to vary. Some parents direct the child's activities, while others concentrate on providing support and encouragement. We often limit our options by seeing Directive Behavior and Supportive Behavior as an either/or dynamic.

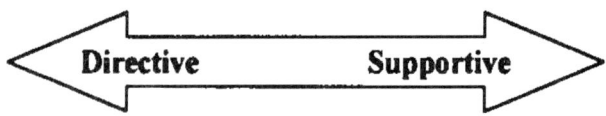

Although we can isolate each set of behaviors for the purposes of defining, each parenting attempt to influence is composed of varying amounts of both Directive and Supportive Behaviors. To use an analogy, it is like seasoning a dish with salt and pepper. There are two distinct elements used in varying degrees to obtain a certain flavor. It is a choice. Some dishes call for more salt and others call for more pepper.

We can choose the amount of Directive Behavior appropriate for the situation. Do I need to use low or high amounts? And the same applies to Supportive Behavior.

PARENT BEHAVIOR

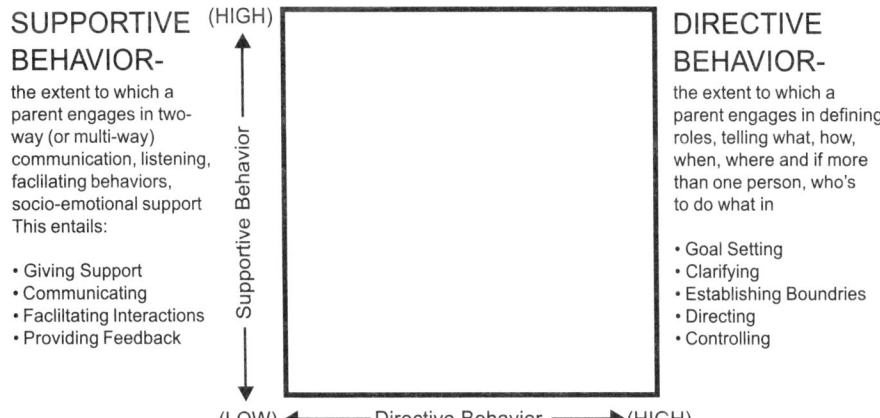

This provides us with an infinite number of possible combinations of Directive and Supportive Behavior. While that is truly representative of "real life," it makes for a cumbersome Model. Effective Parenting is comprised of infinite choices. The good news is that we don't have to determine the exact combination to be a good parent. A useful model begins to unfold by simply dividing each axis in half. This permits each axis of the model to be expressed in ranges. We can now look at Directive Behavior in terms of low-to-moderate and moderate-to-high. The same is true for Supportive Behavior; low-to-moderate and moderate-to-high.

PARENT BEHAVIOR

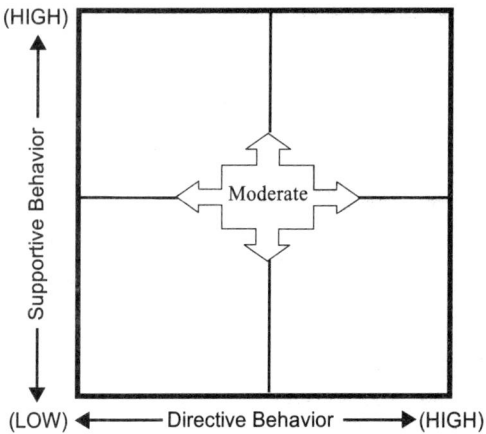

This provides four distinct sets of Parenting Behavior. Each quadrant contains an amount of both Directive and Supportive Behavior. Carefully consider each of the different sets or quadrants. Imagine yourself demonstrating each quadrant one-by-one. What words are used, voice inflections, non-verbal cues and what would the setting be? In addition to defining each style, for the purpose of quick reference, each will be numbered.

PARENT BEHAVIOR

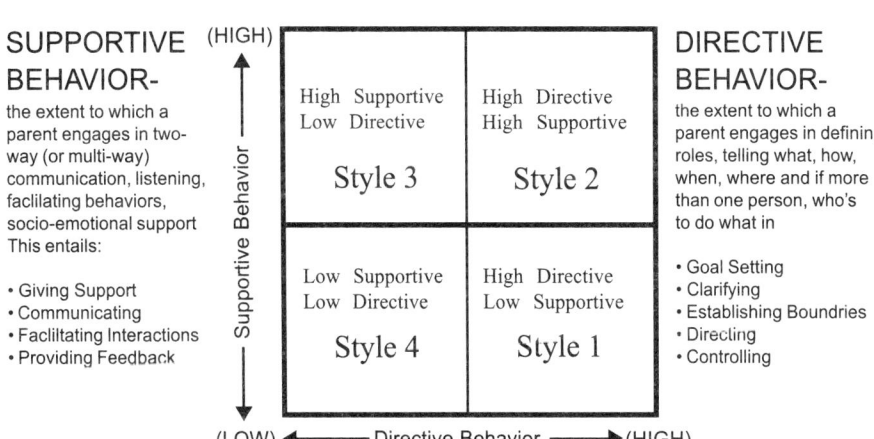

SUPPORTIVE BEHAVIOR-
the extent to which a parent engages in two-way (or multi-way) communication, listening, faclilating behaviors, socio-emotional support
This entails:

• Giving Support
• Communicating
• Facliltating Interactions
• Providing Feedback

DIRECTIVE BEHAVIOR-
the extent to which a parent engages in defining roles, telling what, how, when, where and if more than one person, who's to do what in

• Goal Setting
• Clarifying
• Establishing Boundries
• Directing
• Controlling

Style 1 (S1):

Style 1 (S1) uses a high amount of Directive Behavior combined with a low amount of Supportive Behavior (please note: low not no). This style is called **guiding** because it's a direct approach. The parent provides the specifics of what, where, when, how and if appropriate — with whom in regards to the task or activity.

Example A:

Chris has been driving the family car for several months, but she's only driven during the day. She has stated that she does not like driving at night. However, next Friday night she wants to drive several of her friends to a birthday party. Her Dad takes her aside, sits her down and tells her that night driving is tricky at times and schedules a few practice sessions for the coming week. During the practice drives, he gives specific instructions about the proper techniques for operating the vehicle at night.

Example B:

Pete's Mom decides it's time he became more helpful around the house, starting with the responsibility of clearing the dinner table and doing the dishes. Pete is not very excited about this idea and is resistant. Recognizing that Pete has never attempted this task before, Mom tells him exactly how to clear the table, rinse the dishes before putting them in the dishwasher and wipe the kitchen counters. She watches Pete perform these tasks for the first few nights, providing whatever guidance is needed and even showing Pete how to accomplish the tasks. Notice that in Style 1 the communication is primarily one-way. In both cases, the parents make the decisions, telling their children what to do, when to do it and how to perform the task.

Style 2 (S2):

Style 2 (S2) involves a high amount of both Directive and Supportive Behavior. This style is somewhat less directive than Style 1. It's called **explaining** because the parent is sharing the why's for the desired task.

In Style 2, the parent still wants the task accomplished in a definite time, place and in a specific way. The amount of guidance or Directive Behavior remains high. But the parent adds a high level of support, explaining the reasons for performing the task and giving the child plenty of opportunity to ask questions.

Example A:

Little Mike has had a series of good dental check-ups, mostly because Mom has carefully supervised the nightly brushing. Although Mike is very willing to brush his teeth before bed, he's still not very good at the task. During Mike's last visit the dentist called attention to the effects of not brushing some teeth completely. Mike's Mom monitors his brushing closely, making sure he brushes thoroughly, repeating the instructions and even modeling the right techniques, and praising his efforts.

Example B:

It's Sunday and company is coming, but the front porch needs sweeping and Mom decides that Stephanie should do the job. Stephanie is usually cooperative and Mom expects that her daughter will pitch in willingly. "Stephanie, I need your help," she says. "We're having company today and the front porch needs cleaning. If I explain what needs to be done could you help with this task?"

Style 3 (S3):

Style 3 (S3) uses high amounts of Supportive Behavior, but low amounts of Directive Behavior. It's called **encouraging** because the parent and child now share the decision-making through two-way communication. The parent is actively listening, praising and asking questions to encourage the child to communicate thoughts, feelings and ideas.

The major difference between Style 3 and Styles 1 and 2 is that the decision-making has switched from parent to child, as has much of the ownership of the outcomes. In Styles 1 and 2, the parent controls the decision or the issue, and often is more interested in the outcome or process than the child. In Style 3, the child provides most of the what, where, when, how and with whom surrounding the issue. They "own" the outcomes and accept their responsibility.

Example A:

Johnny's job is to help with the Saturday family chores. Dad notices that the garage needs a general clean up. At breakfast Dad says, "Johnny, the yard looks great. I think today's a good day for cleaning the garage. I've noticed we have been growing quite a mess out there. What do you think about tackling this one?"

Example B:

The Sanchez teenagers are going to be left on their own while their parents attend an out of town sales meeting. A few days before the big trip, Mom calls the gang together to say, "You know Dad and I are going to be gone again until the weekend and you're on your own. Your father and I have a lot of confidence in you and we know you'll keep the house rules while we're away. How do you think you should arrange the meals and other chores?"

Style 4 (S4):

Style 4 involves low amounts of both Supportive Behavior and Directive Behavior — this still involves conversation and praise. Unlike Style 3 where praise needs to be specific, Style 4 praise seems to be more generalized and a bit more infrequent. The low amounts of Directive Behavior are often accomplished by simple exchanges of ideas regarding how things are going and observing. The important point here is both sets of behavior are low amounts — not NO!

Example A:

On Thursday, Ben's father reminds him that the family is leaving Saturday morning for a trip to the desert and that he should have the lawn mowed before they go. "Just let me know when the job's done," says Dad.

Example B:

Carrie and Bill are college sophomores who earned money during the summer to finance their social activities, something they have done since their senior year in high school. Since September, they have not called for any monetary help from their parents. During a telephone call regarding next semester's tuition Mom says, "Dad and I can handle the tuition just fine, I've got to tell you how glad we are to see you're both doing O.K. with money for personal activities."

Before moving on to other elements of the Situational Parenting® Model there is a final key factor regarding styles. A style is a pattern of behaviors that the parent engages in *as perceived by the child.* It is not how we intend to act or how we thought we acted that counts. At least, not nearly as much as how the child experiences our behavior.

Chapter Three
Readiness

There are many variables that come together (sometimes collide) in parenting. Of all the influences we could mention, none is more important than the relationship between a parent and a child. In Chapter Two, we began to look at Parenting styles. In this chapter we will explore the child's behavior. What is it about them that we need to respond to?

Let's revisit Andrew and Sally from the previous chapter. Andrew didn't know the mechanics of tying a tie. However, he may be very dependable in terms of playing in the yard and staying out of the street. Sally, although adept at mowing the lawn, may be unwilling to do certain homework assignments. And so it goes with everyone. We all have an array of diverse tasks, responsibilities and abilities. That is why no **one style** will work for us and why parenting is not only the most important job in the world, but also one of the most difficult.

To be fair, and to meet Sally and Andrew's diverse needs, we have to be task specific. What this means is what particular activity, responsibility, problem, goal or task are we trying to influence? There are times when really focusing on a specific task is challenging. When talking to Sally on how she is doing with keeping her room clean I may be able to generalize and get a good picture of her performance.

Asking myself the same question regarding Andrew may not prove as helpful. Andrew may do well with keeping his toys picked up and dirty clothes in the hamper. However, he just can't manage to make his bed (remember he is seven). If I start talking to Andrew with the general task of keeping his room clean when I am really focused on making his bed neatly, we will be on two different wave lengths with two different pictures of performance. We need to be *task specific*.

Now that we have focused on the task, the next step is to diagnose (figure out) where the child is in relation to the task. Again, an infinite number of possibilities and variables exist. Through our decades of leadership training we have found that once you have plowed your way through piles of academic studies and consultant observations you usually end up with some basic fundamental touchstones. So it is in parenting. How **ready** is the child for the task? It is a great question and one, as parents, we frequently ask, once we are willing to slow down and think before we act. Readiness is composed of two interacting variables — ability and willingness.

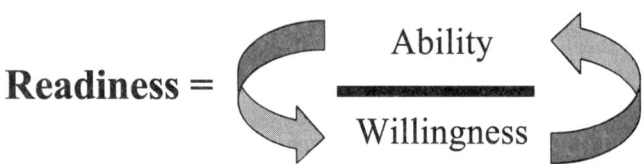

Readiness = $\dfrac{\text{Ability}}{\text{Willingness}}$

Readiness is determined by the extent that the child is demonstrating levels of ability and levels of willingness. This is about the task, not the child. It's important to recognize that readiness is not a personal characteristic. It's not an evaluation of a child's traits, values, worth, etc. Readiness is simply the manner in which a child performs a particular task.

Taking another look at Andrew and the task of tying his tie. His level of ability was low (hanging to the side in several knots you have never seen before) and his level of willingness was low, particularly at the end of the scene (crying).

Ability and willingness are extremely interactive; meaning a change in one can have a significant impact on the other. The impact of this interactivity is a very individual dynamic. With some children, having difficulty or having a hard time with something can create a great deal of frustration and destroy their previous willingness to try. "I don't want to do this," "I hate this," or "Do this for me," becomes the resultant cries. While another child in the very same circumstance will start over or plow straight through the task at hand, alone or with a request for help.

Ability and willingness are great summary terms, each contain a number of helpful clues that increase our probability of making an accurate "readiness" diagnosis.

Child Readiness

Presently demonstrating...

Ability

Ability is a child's *demonstrated* skill in doing something. Children who have an ability in a particular area demonstrate the knowledge, experience and skill to do tasks in that area with minimal direction from others.

We measure ability in terms of "how much" knowledge, experience and skill we can observe. It is important not to fall into the trap of looking at skills as present or missing. Consider ability in terms of degrees. For example, your daughter may have low levels of ability when it comes to doing certain homework assignments; some ability in helping with particular household chores; quite a bit of ability in terms of soccer; and a great deal of ability in helping others resolve their differences.

Perhaps the most frequent error made in correctly diagnosing ability is impacting knowledge and assuming the child has developed skills. If you have ever provided clear directions, backed off and then discovered the child could not perform, you have experienced this trap. Impacting knowledge about what and how something "should" be done does not ensure skill.

Willingness

Willingness is a child's demonstrated motivation, confidence and commitment to do something. Children who are willing to perform a certain task have confidence, commitment and motivation and they will probably plunge in with enthusiasm when asked to do it.

Willingness indicators can be easily misdiagnosed with devastating results. This is particularly true when there is an apparent lack of willingness – unwilling. Children, just like adults, can be insecure, uncertain, frustrated or confused over a certain task. The difference between unmotivated and insecure is significant and so is the appropriate response from the parent.

It is important to remember that willingness is task specific too. We measure willingness in terms of "how often" we observe it. For example, Bobby may seldom be willing to take his younger brother along to the ball field; occasionally willing to take out the garbage; usually willing to go shopping with his mother; and always willing to watch a ball game on TV.

Important to the definition of ability and willingness is the word **demonstrated**. Parents need to judge readiness in terms of the behavior they see. Without **demonstrated** ability, we're only dealing with potential or holding the child accountable for what we think they *should* be able to do. Without **demonstrated** ability, we're dealing with simple intent without action.

There is also a frequent trap for misdiagnosis of willingness. It is easy to mistake insecurity for unmotivated or unwilling. Part of the reason is that insecurity can take many forms. It can be unclear, uncertain, apprehensive, overwhelmed and/or afraid. When the child is exhibiting any of these behaviors with a degree of energy it often comes across as resisting or just not wanting to do what is asked of them. This dynamic is compounded when the child concludes that it is more socially acceptable to act unmotivated than to be seen as insecure. Most children get this message from siblings and peers at a very early age.

Now that we have defined these two dynamics we can begin to plot them. As stated, readiness is displayed in degrees or ranges.

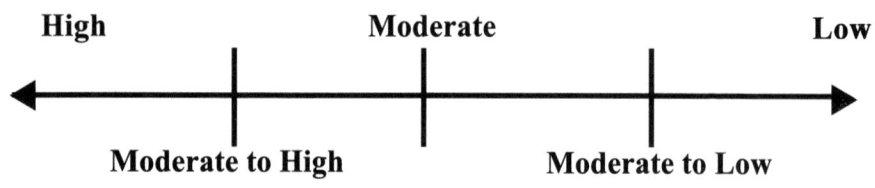

This provides us with four ranges of Child Readiness. Although we are about to sequentially number each level, we do so with a word of caution. Readiness is dynamic. People don't develop or regress in readiness based on our number system.

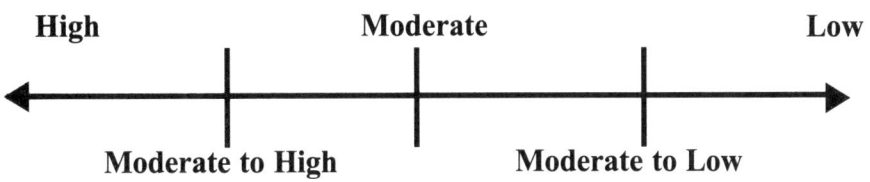

The remainder of this chapter is dedicated to putting faces and real people on each of these readiness factors. You are invited to stop reading after each point or paragraph until you can see pictures of real children in real situations and make our words come to life. On to readiness levels...

Unable and Unwilling:

The child is unable to perform the task or is capable but not willing to demonstrate ability, commitment or motivation. Example: Terry cannot seem to remember to put her toys away no matter how often her mother tells her to do so. When confronted with a living room floor covered with toys, her usual response is "I forgot." If pressed to do so however, she finally does put them away but does a poor job.

or

Unable and Insecure:

The child is unable to perform the task and lacks confidence. Example: Brandy has always been a very successful student. This is her first year in Algebra and unknown to you, things are not going well. She has failed several of her assignments and did poorly on her quiz. Out of sheer frustration she has stopped making any attempts on her homework.

Readiness Level One (R1):

Child Readiness

HIGH	MODERATE		LOW
R4	R3	R2	R1
			Unable and Unwilling or Insecure

Unable but Willing

The child has low-to-moderate ability, but is motivated and is making an effort. Example: Marcos is seven and for his recent birthday you decided to make his dream come true, Marcos now has Skamp, a loving little puppy. When Marcos is home, Skamp has his undivided attention. However, Marcos feeds Skamp off schedule and with varying amounts of food and there seems to be a bit of a timing issue taking Skamp for his needed walks.

or

Unable but Confident:

The child is demonstrating moderate-to-low skills, but shows confidence. The confidence can be self-confidence or confidence and feeling safe with you there to help. Example: You have started to teach Pat to swim and this is the first day in the big pool. After an hour of successful play and small amounts of actual lesson, Pat wants to try jumping into the pool, but only from the side. After a few seconds of dancing in place, Pat says, "Okay, I'm ready, you can catch me now."

Readiness Level Two (R2):

Child Readiness

HIGH	MODERATE		LOW
R4	R3	R2	R1
		Unable but Willing or Confident	Unable and Unwilling or Insecure

Able but Unwilling:

The child is demonstrating moderate levels of ability but is clearly not motivated to do the task. Example: Connie is fifteen and her younger brother Timmy is seven. Connie has taken several courses offered through the school for babysitting. She has also been trained in first aid. Several of your neighbors have expressed a great deal of satisfaction with her ability and use her services frequently. Although she has watched Timmy a number of times in the past (unpaid) she now resists and expresses her desire to no longer "get stuck" watching him.

or

Able but Insecure:

The child has the ability to perform the task, but is insecure about doing it alone. Example: Jason has just approached you and states, "Dad I need to talk with you." He tells you that while playing in the living room with his younger brother, he knocked Mom's favorite vase off the end table and it broke. Jason accepts responsibility and asks, "What am I going to say to Mom?"

Readiness Level Three (R3):

Child Readiness

HIGH	MODERATE		LOW
R4	R3	R2	R1
	Able but Unwilling or Insecure	Unable but Willing or Confident	Unable and Unwilling or Insecure

Able and Willing and Confident

Randy is twelve and the self proclaimed Taco King. About once a week he prepares a complete dinner. He has expanded the meal to include green salad, both chicken and beef tacos and recently introduced a variety of salsas.

Readiness Level Four (R4):

Child Readiness

HIGH	MODERATE		LOW
R4	R3	R2	R1
Able and Willing & Confident	Able but Unwilling or Insecure	Unable but Willing or Confident	Unable and Unwilling or Insecure

Readiness Cue Library

To enhance our understanding of Readiness it is necessary to build a library of cues for each of the four levels. In the following pages we have provided a collection of cues meant only as a starting point. The best cues for you will come from thinking about your own children and how they act during certain situations. Again, the invitation is offered to move slowly through the next few pages. Take the time to personalize each readiness level. To aid in the quest for understanding readiness, the next few pages will add another layer of cues for each of the four levels.

READINESS LEVEL ONE (R1):

R4	R3	R2	R1

Unable & Unwilling or Insecure

Indicators:
- Not performing task to acceptable level
- Intimidated by task
- Unclear about directions
- Procrastinating
- Unfinished tasks
- Avoidance "passing the buck'
- Defensiveness or discomfort

At the core of Readiness Level One (R1) is the issue of performance. The child cannot or will not demonstrate ability. Setting aside those rare moments of frustration and impatience, parents do a relatively good job of recognizing the "cannot" situations as beyond the child's control. In these settings the child gives strong signals of apprehension or fear. Particularly when the child is young, we have little difficulty demonstrating compassion and seeing our parental role as one of helping.

The "will not" episodes seem to be more difficult, perhaps because we feel (and sometimes we are) challenged. Much of a child's early life is the discovery of boundaries. At some point, they will demonstrate their defiance through "don't want to," "lack of desire to do what we want or when we want it" or "not at all." Some children learn to articulate this in a way that is acceptable, others resort to temper tantrums. This is when the defiance becomes more important than the task.

For the purpose of brevity R1 works fine. For the purpose of understanding and collecting cues we need to break R1 into two distinct combinations of Unable and Unwilling and Unable and Insecure.

READINESS LEVEL ONE (R1)

Unable & Unwilling
- Defensive, argumentative, complaining
- Late completion of task
- Performance only to exact request
- Intense frustration, negative expressions

Unable & Insecure
- Body language will express discomfort: furrowed brow, shoulders lowered, leaning back
- Confused, unclear
- Afraid of possible outcomes
- Fear of failure

Readiness Level Two (R2) is where most of the early stages of the learning cycle takes place. In fact, for most tasks, in a healthy environment this is the starting point for development, not in R1. Here, children have a contagious enthusiasm for learning. This is the source of "how does it work," "show me how to," "can you teach me to," "I want to try to" and the endless list of "why" questions. R2 more than any other level needs to be accepted, encouraged and nurtured. The caution here is to realize that responding appropriately to this Readiness Level sets a critical precedence for future learning opportunities.

READINESS LEVEL TWO (R2):

R4	R3	**R2**	R1

Unable & Willing or Confident

Indicators:
- Anxious or excited
- Interested & responsive
- Demonstrating moderate ability
- Receptive to input
- Attentive
- Enthusiastic
- New task - no experience

Confidence, desire and motivation are powerful human factors. Self-help books have been written on the single complex issue of building self-esteem. As a parent we need to look at this Readiness Level as a precious and fragile gift from the child. When children are predominantly at this level there exists an unspoken psychological contract. The contract is predicated on several fragile issues:

- Every action on the parents' part conveys they mean the child no harm. That you and your learning are safe with me.
- There is no place for blame, fault or guilt in learning.
- Not knowing is a time for exploration and discovery.
- Desire to learn is as important as the accomplishment.
- Your self-esteem is ours to build.

READINESS LEVEL TWO (R2)

Unable & Willing or Confident
- Fast verbal pace; intense
- Seeks clarity
- Nodding head, "yes, I know" type comments, eager
- Answers questions superficially
- Accepting of tasks
- Quick to act
- Pre-occupied with outcomes versus increments

In Readiness Level Three (R3) things have changed. The issue, and therefore the timing and setting belong more to the child. The key is to be able to switch from action and doing to one of sensitivity to Readiness Cues. Patience, empathy, listening and encouragement are the needs of the R3. We can actually become cue insensitive to this particular Readiness Level. In the first two Readiness Levels it is most often the parent that initiates the conversation and it is usually based on how much time we have and where our mind is.

READINESS LEVEL THREE (R3):

R4	R3	R2	R1

Able & Unwilling or Insecure

Indicators:
- First time "solo" performance
- Lacks confidence and experience
- Needs feedback and encouragement
- Previously demonstrated knowledge & skill
- Performance slipping - upset about things

In R3 we have two distinctions again; Able but Unwilling or Able but Insecure. The child is performing at moderate-to-high levels so ability is not the issue. The cues we need to develop are in relation to confidence, commitment and motivation. If the issue seems to be centered around losing desire while still performing, we are probably looking at slippage in performance. High probability is that the child has previously achieved higher levels of performance on this task. Cues such as overwhelmed, tired, unappreciated and not feeling as good about success or performance has become punishing for the child.

Able but insecure applies more when the child is developing or has recently acquired a set of skills with help from others. Often the insecurity is due to factors seemingly outside of the performance issue. "I can do this at home when I practice, but other people will be there…." It is difficult for many people to express insecurity or apprehension and the cues become personal and subtle.

READINESS LEVEL THREE (R3)

Able & Unwilling
- Hesitant or resistant
- Feels over obligated & over extended
- Seeks reinforcement
- Performance is somehow punishing

Able & Insecure
- Questions own ability
- Focuses on potential problems
- Lacks self esteem
- Encourages parent to stay involved

If we could sit down together and enjoy a lengthy conversation about each of the Readiness Levels, Readiness Level Four (R4) would be the shortest. The following cues, interestingly enough, seem to apply to all age groups. But there are some misconceptions that divert us from enjoying R4. First, don't wait for perfection to celebrate the accomplishment of getting to this level. We are talking about high levels of performance not perfection.

READINESS LEVEL FOUR (R4):

R4	R3	R2	R1

<u>Able & Willing & Confident</u>
- Keeps parent informed of progress
- Makes efficient use of resources
- Responsive to suggestions
- Knowledgeable; shares information and innovation
- Volunteers help
- Shares creative ideas
- "Takes-charge" of responsibilities
- Completes responsibilities on time and perhaps early

Second, when children reach this level for a task, parents often refrain from acknowledging the accomplishment and immediately announce another activity or issue that needs to be worked on. Third, R4 is not some ultimate destination that we want our children to achieve for all their activities. Admittedly there are days when responding to any other Readiness Level does not seem humanly possible. The fact is we, parents and children, function at a variety of Readiness Levels for the many different tasks and responsibilities that we have. As learning, living beings we need new challenges.

Note:
Occasionally we meet resistance to the volume of information regarding Readiness Levels. Often this is expressed as, "Do we really have to make figuring out what is going on with the child such a process?" Our best answer is "yes." And that it is something that as parents, we have been doing all along, but without a structure with which to assemble the cues.

See if this meets with your experience — You are now home with your newborn, basking in the glow of wonderment over this blessed miracle. About three days later you sit holding this precious gift as it discovers its' lungs. For an hour, the baby discovers its' lungs. You sit there with mounting frustration and as tears fill your eyes you ask, "What do you need? I'd do anything for you, I just don't know what you need." That is when you first discovered readiness (not in this book).

Our children are like mirrors
They reflect our attitudes and behaviors in life.

Chapter Four
The Model

Attitude vs. Behavior

When looking at Parenting Styles, the focus is on behavior. There's a distinct difference between behavior and attitude. Behavior is what parents say and do. Attitudes are feelings, values, concerns for or against something.

It's sometimes difficult to tell the difference between a behavior and an attitude. People who have similar attitudes (value sets) about something may engage in a variety of behaviors. For example, parents who have a high concern for problems in schoolwork can act in different ways. Some may avoid the issue altogether. Others may be sympathetic and encouraging about the problems. Still others, with the same attitude, get actively involved in their children's homework assignments. In these cases the same high concern evoked different behaviors. It's our behavior that affects others, not our attitudes. It is the behavior the child sees, not the attitude that drove it.

Parents need to be concerned for both their children and the end results of the children's actions. To capitalize on this concern, a number of Parenting Styles must be used to adapt to the different situations or problems parents face.

For example, a father loves both of his teenage children equally. That is, he has the same attitude toward each of them. However, he recognizes that each child has a different level of ability and motivation toward schoolwork. Tony usually gets all his assignments done on time, while Gerry usually produces too little, too late. As a result, Tony's grades are respectable while Gerry is barely passing.

Although his attitude is the same toward both children, Dad's behavior varies with each of them. With Tony, he can simply observe the good performance and give an occasional "attaboy" to let Tony know he's interested in the boy's success. But with Gerry, the father needs to give plenty of hands-on-guidance, sometimes assisting with the assignments and checking frequently to see how she is doing.

Likewise, children can differ greatly in their ability and readiness to perform certain tasks. Take Tom, a high school junior, who is very serious about his commitment to football. During the summer, Tom sets his own practice schedule, watches his weight and gets a good night's sleep. In this area, Tom needs very little supervision or guidance.

However, this is not the case in terms of Tom's ability to get along with others. Even with his close friends, Tom is often at the center of disagreements, and some of the guys no longer hang out with him. Tom's readiness to handle these situations is low; therefore, he still needs parental guidance and supervision to learn how to deal effectively with his peers.

In football, Tom is ready to act responsibly; in his social relationships, Tom is not ready to take responsibility to act appropriately. Thus, Tom's parents need to vary their styles according to their son's needs. The key to successful and effective parenting is to adjust the Parenting Style to the readiness needs of the child for the specific task at hand.

Parenting Style:

In Chapter Two, we portrayed the four Parenting Styles in a two-dimensional model, by plotting Directive Behavior on one axis and Supportive Behavior on another. Then we developed the four basic Parenting Styles; each contained in a separate quadrant of the model.

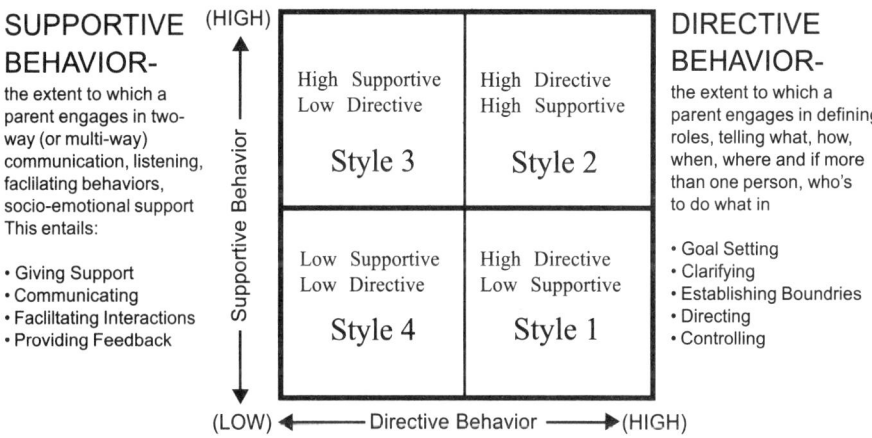

Chapter Three explored variations of Ready, Willing and Able. Recall that within each of the four Readiness Levels there exists a variety of interacting elements. And that each child functions at a variety of Readiness Levels, depending on the task we are focusing upon. It is also important to recognize the very personal and unique manner we all display readiness.

Child Readiness

HIGH	MODERATE		LOW
R4	R3	R2	R1
Able and Willing & Confident	Able but Unwilling or Insecure	Unable but Willing or Confident	Unable and Unwilling or Insecure

We can isolate Parent Behavior and Child Readiness for the purpose of discussion and explanation. In real life, the two are forever intertwined. The success and effectiveness of the parenting attempt to influence is largely determined by the accuracy of matching the Parenting Style to the Readiness Level of the child for *a specific task*. It is the interface of style and readiness that becomes the Situational Parenting® Model. There are three steps to using the model:

1. Identify the specific task, job, or activity.
2. Assess the readiness of the child for this specific task.
3. Select the matching Parenting Behaviors that meet the needs of the child.

Step 1:

It is hard to maintain your focus on instructing the child on how to unstick a stuck zipper when you are trying to shape a life, particularly when it is your offspring. But that is exactly the challenge. As parents we seem to want big fixes, to have more than the moment at hand in mind. And indeed what we do in the moment may have profound impact on the future. That is precisely why we need to maintain our focus on the job before us.

Another distraction comes in the form of desire for convenience. It would be nice to be able to generalize and still be accurate. For example, it would be convenient to look at all forms of homework as a task. The probability is that the child will display varying levels of readiness by subject and type of homework (does better at math than social studies, completes nightly assignments well, but has difficulty with large projects, does the reading, but can't write the book report, etc.).

Step 2:

Take the time (usually only takes a matter of seconds) to really diagnose Readiness Levels. It is too easy to fall into the activity trap of acting before really thinking. When we focus on what we are going to do or on the outcome, we often forget this important step. It is like providing a great answer to the wrong question. Diagnosing readiness is the key to selecting the right set of Parenting Behaviors. If you reread any chapter of this book, let it be Chapter Three. Develop your own list of real life ability and willingness indicators for your child. Give careful consideration to the interaction of ability and willingness as it pertains to the child and the specific task at hand. Remember this interaction is a very personal variable.

Step 3:

Only now do we design how we respond to the child's needs. This is a matching process of varying the amounts of Directive Behavior and Supportive Behavior to the degrees of ability and willingness the child is demonstrating for the task at hand.

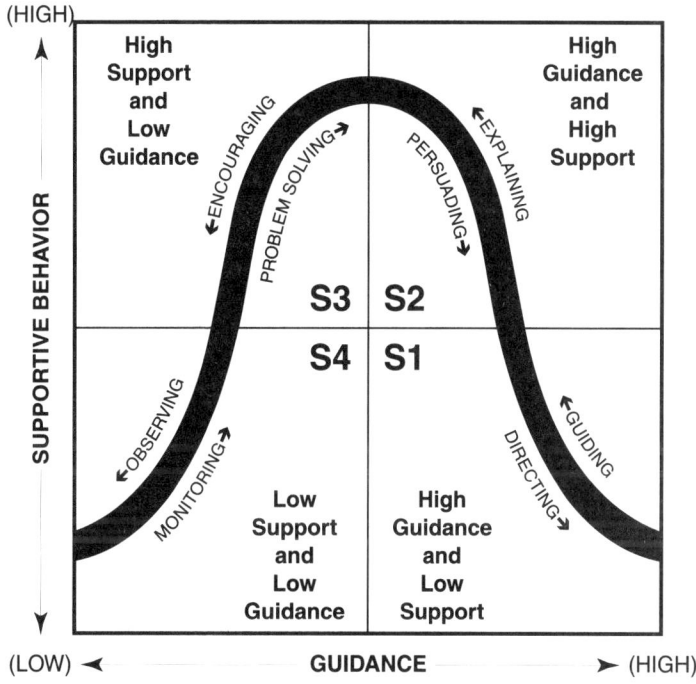

The Matching Process

Style 1 (S1) and Readiness Level 1 (R1)

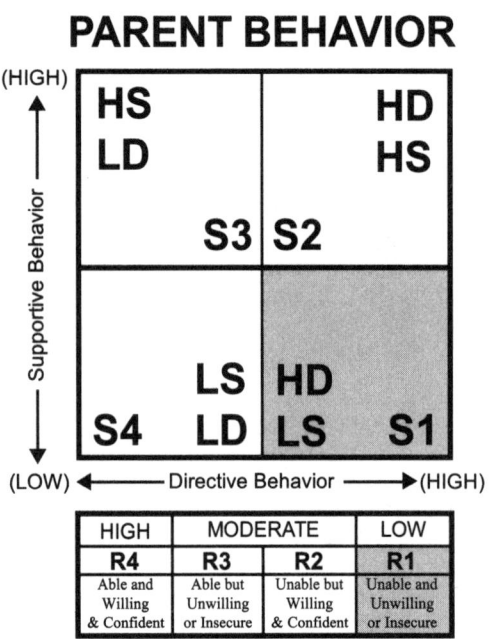

The R1 Situation:

Marty does not want to put his toys away, and when asked, usually converts a messy bedroom into a messier closet. His response to the last couple of attempts has been to toss or kick his toys into the closet and proclaim that "it's good enough."

Since Marty is neither able (has not yet performed at an acceptable level) nor motivated (and is in fact just a bit defiant) to put his toys away, the appropriate style is S1, with high directive or guidance and low (not no) support.

S1 should come across to Marty as:

Guiding or Directing or Establishing or Telling

It is important not to come across as:

Demanding or Demeaning or Dominating or Attacking

S1 Matching Style:

An effective style:

"Before you watch any TV, Marty, you need to put your toys away. Today things are going to be put back carefully and neatly. Your coloring books go on the shelf by the window. (Pause for compliance.) Now the train goes in the chest in your closet. We can finish making your room nice and neat by putting the building blocks in the box on the patio."

At the risk of being redundant, consider how the child is experiencing the style, not how you intend to come across. It is easy for S1 to become unnecessarily emotionally charged. As such, our intended guiding is perceived as demanding or demeaning.

Style 2 (S2) and Readiness Level 2 (R2)

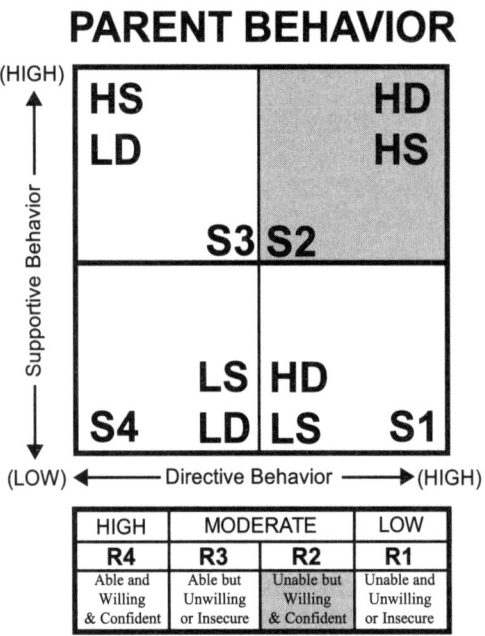

The R2 Situation:

Sarah is eager to help Dad build the perfect birdhouse. This is Sarah's first wood working project and she can hardly contain her excitement. Dad cut out all the pieces last night. It is now time to assemble the masterpiece.

The S2 Matching Style:

Since Sarah is willing to learn, but unable to use a hammer properly, the appropriate style is S2, using high amounts of both guidance and support. Notice how the father explains why safety and technique are important.

S2 should come across to Sarah as:

Explaining or Persuading or Clarifying or Convincing

Not as:
Manipulating or Preaching or Defending or Rationalizing

An effective style:

"Okay Sarah, are you as excited as I am about putting your birdhouse together?" Sarah responds with a big smile and a nod of her head. "Now you said you wanted to build the house so I'm going to show you exactly how to use a hammer. Take one of these nails and hold it with the point end on the piece of wood. That's right, you placed it right in the middle of the board. That makes it much safer and easier to hammer the nail. Let's use this smaller hammer because we have small nails. You'll find the hammer easier to use if you place your hand right here on the handle.

An ineffective style:

"Now we're going to learn to hammer nails. Are you sure you still want to help with this?" Sarah nods her head yes as a smile appears. "You have the pieces right there on the bench, let's see you put it together." Sarah executes the first tap of the hammer safely; the second blow of the hammer sends the nail flying and the boards falling over. Dad immediately takes the hammer; "Okay you are going to hurt yourself using the hammer that way. Let me show you how to put it together properly.

Style S3 (S3) and Readiness Level 3 (R3)

PARENT BEHAVIOR

	HIGH	MODERATE		LOW
	R4	**R3**	**R2**	**R1**
	Able and Willing & Confident	Able but Unwilling or Insecure	Unable but Willing & Confident	Unable and Unwilling or Insecure

The R3 Situation:

Mark has worked very hard on a science project. He has done an exceptional job researching and preparing his project for display. He created a device that lights up in the back window of the car if the seat belts are not connected. His efforts have been rewarded and what was once excitement has turned into serious apprehension. Mark has been selected to represent his class in the school's science fair. He exclaims to his Mom, "Everyone in the school is going to be looking at my project!"

The S3 Matching Style:

Mark has completed the knowledge and skill side of the science fair. What he doesn't need is guidance and direction. Mark is having butterflies and perhaps a little stage fright over the "show" part of the science fair. Supportive Behavior to talk through the apprehension and a bit of praise regarding his accomplishment will help Mark put things in perspective and celebrate his success.

S3 should come across to Mark as:

Encouraging or Problem-Solving or Listening or Participating

Not as:

Patronizing or Placating or Condescending or Pacifying

An effective style:

"Mark, you sound concerned, tell me why being in the fair bothers you."

"I'm going to look like a dork," says Mark.

Mom asks, "Because you're in the fair?"

Mark replies, "No, not because I'm in the fair, I wanted that. You don't know what some of the other projects are like. One kid made a robot that actually moves."

Mom responds, "Is your concern about being compared to the work of the other students?"

"It's not a competition Mom, but kids always compare. This year there are a lot of great projects," says Mark.

"Mark, I know how hard you worked on your project. You amazed me with the facts you had on the number and severity of damage in accidents when people don't wear seat belts. It sounds like given what you say about other projects, and how good yours is, this is going to be one exciting science fair. Have you congratulated any of the other winners?"

An ineffective style:

"Well, Mark, didn't you know that there was going to be a science fair?"

Mark replies, "Of course I did, I just wasn't expecting to make it with my project."

Mom says, "I really wish you wouldn't underestimate yourself so much, you did a fine job, you ought to be proud and have more confidence in your work. I don't understand why you don't want to be in the science fair. Why don't you want to show your project?" Mark walks off saying, "It isn't about the dumb fair."

Style S4 (S4) and Readiness Level 4 (R4)

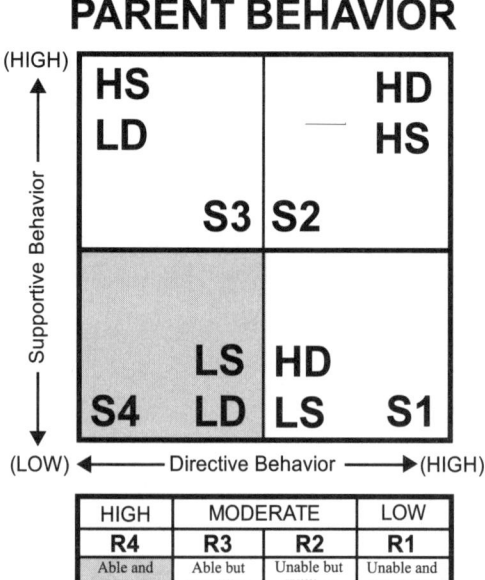

The R4 Situation:

Pat is extremely conscientious about completing homework assignments. You have been pleased with her consistent display of self discipline and responsibility. According to the feedback on today's report from Pat's teachers, they too see the effort and fine results.

The S4 Matching Style:

Since Pat is perfectly capable and very committed to completing assigned homework, the most appropriate Parenting Style is S4, using low amounts of guidance and support. (Note that self-motivated and self-directed people do not need a lot of external praise and encouragement – they get most of their reinforcement from task accomplishment.)

S4 should come across to Pat as:

Observing or Monitoring or Entrusting or Assigning

Not as:

Abandoning or Ignoring or Avoiding or Withdrawing

An effective style:

"Hey Pat, I am really proud of the way you keep so focused on your homework. Are you aware of how good your study habits are?"

An ineffective style:

"At least you're keeping up with your homework, that makes one less thing I have to worry about."

How do I know when to change Parenting Styles? How can I help my child become more responsible? You want to increase your children's readiness for the activities they'll have to face in life. And as the Situational Parenting® Model illustrates, increasing levels of readiness requires different Parenting Styles. In the next chapter, we'll address the question of changing Parenting Styles in order to help your child grow in readiness. We'll show you how you can use the Situational Parenting® Model to help your children along a path toward independence.

Choosing the Right Style for the Situation

The examples given in this chapter should provide you with pictures of what the four Parenting Styles sound/look like. S1 is characterized by Direct Guidance with low input from the child. S2 still relies heavily on guidance, but allows the child to share in the parent's reason for wanting the task done. S3 shifts decision-making regarding the task to more of a joint relationship, but the parent is still there to provide encouragement and help. S4 hands responsibility for getting the task done over to the child, with the parent functioning as an observer, providing low amounts of occasional support. Consider the following ... *We can only feel independent once we feel sufficiently connected to other people.*

Acceptance

How do we ensure the acceptance of, or the reception to, the use of a Parenting Style? Let's start with the suggestion that has the highest degree of utility. Make sure you are matching your style to the Readiness Level of the task at hand. When style use and readiness match there is a perceptual harmony. Things feel right. Even when the child may not like the style they are receiving, they can understand how their behavior has elicited yours. Children are constantly trying to make sense out of the world, and we leverage this desire for understanding by being predictable. We want the child to see that we respond to them. Our behavior is driven by what they need from us.

A helpful technique to increase receptivity to a style is to let the child experience being the one to deliver it. We suggest that you actually create opportunities for the child to use the different influence (parenting) styles. As you continue reading this section remember that the goal is for the child to learn to use a style, it has no bearing on your real readiness.

A frequent use of Style 1 is in situations that are procedural and compliance is really non-negotiable such as when we get in the car, we all buckle our seat belts, lock the door and check the rear view mirror. Let the child run down this checklist and be sure to thank them when they point out that you forgot a step. This teaches the child that the style is about safety and not a message to the person about them as a person. That Style 1 can be delivered in a pleasant manner and the recipient of the style can accept the direction with grace and maybe even gratitude.

Moving on to Style 2...this is both a great teaching style and a problem solving style. It is also a wonderful place to answer the question, "why," which endlessly enters a young child's mind. Find an opportunity to have the child teach you something (finger-paint, make a snack, math, etc.).

A particular favorite for Style 3 is sharing with the child something you would like to do for them. Let them know you would like their encouragement and to spend a few minutes together sharing your ideas. During the interaction be responsive to any display of questioning technique and active listening. End the conversation with praise or some expression to capture the positive exchange.

An important transition happens in Style 4. The majority of the behavior is on the follower's (or child's) part as the R4. A sure sign of an R4 is to keep the parent informed of progress, problems and accomplishments. To help teach a child to use S4 you must be the best possible R4. Select an activity that the child asks you to do. Be sure it is one that will provide several points to give an update on progress and has a clearly understood outcome or ending.

Through guidance and support our children will gain their independence as their ability and willingness grow stronger. However, keep in mind that things can happen, children will regress, and as parents you will have to step in to prevent further slippage, but more on that in Chapter Six.

Seek to shape outwardly
Whatever moves the heart of the child
Because even the child's love can decay
If not nourished carefully.

Chapter Five
Building Success and Self Esteem

This chapter is about managing small steps. In sorting through our lives for examples and content in preparation for this chapter it became increasingly apparent that building success and self-esteem are the sources of great parenting memories (the big and small successes). In reflection we rediscovered the times when our "heart was in our throat" and the times "that warmed our hearts." This is about celebrating small accomplishments, enjoying learning and at times being a proud spectator as our children claim a well deserved moment of growth for themselves.

Throughout this book we have attempted to focus on the interaction or the moment at hand in the belief that in doing so the larger picture will be nurtured and healthy. These two dynamics – the moment at hand and the larger picture – require a delicate balancing act. We ask your patience while we indulge ourselves with another analogy. Picture a glass of water about three-quarters full (the larger picture). You are tasked with filling this glass with an eyedropper, one-drop at a time (the moment at hand).

You can fill your dropper from a number of different cups of colored dye. Your goal is to end up with a full glass of rose colored water.

You accomplish this drop by drop and by varying the color selections you make to achieve the final effect. These incremental one-by-one drops create that final result. As parents we are often clearer about the big picture than we are at seeing the small steps that contribute to getting us there.

As parents, we have a responsibility to help children "grow" in terms of their readiness to take responsibility for performing tasks; to manage those small steps toward increasing responsibility. That's how we contribute to a child's growth and development toward becoming mature, responsible and self-motivated adults. We need to be catalysts for that growth and assist them in acquiring readiness.

Perhaps the first question to ask is, "Which areas of my child's life do I want to influence?" The answer to this question changes, as the child changes. Parents of pre-school children might be more concerned about teaching table manners, dressing themselves and so on. As the children get older, the areas of life parents attempt to influence grow more complicated. Social interactions, schoolwork, respect for others and responsibility for personal possessions (cars, clothes, etc.) come into play.

Goal setting is a simple process. Once we know exactly what we want a child to do, we have to communicate the goal to the child. Sometimes we need to describe what good behavior looks like, so there won't be any misunderstandings. Some parents may write the goals on a piece of paper as a ready reference for the child.

Once we have determined what area we want to influence, we must clearly specify what our expectations are so that everyone understands. It's not enough to tell your child that you want him to keep his room clean, you need to specify what a clean room looks like.

Remember Andrew? Keeping in mind that he's only seven, would you have greater success if you say, "I want you to make sure your bed is made, your toys are picked up off the floor, your wastepaper basket is empty and your clothes are neatly put away ." Or would you do better to show Andrew by example what you mean by "neatly" in order that you both understand what is expected.

Also, it's important that a child living with both parents not get mixed messages regarding these expectations. If one parent says that the room is neat and the other says it's a mess the child will be confused. Parents cannot change or develop a child's behavior in an area where expectations are unclear.

As time passes, effective parents will review the goals with the child and give feedback, just as a supervisor will frequently let employees know how they're doing toward agreed-upon goals. This process provides opportunity to see whether the child's behavior is truly directed toward the goals you have set.

The Need for Positive Reinforcement

Parents should remember that no one, including themselves, learns how to do anything all at once. We learn a little bit at a time. Because of this, when a parent wants a child to do something completely new, the parent should reward the slightest progress the child makes in the desired direction. This is called **positive reinforcement**.

Do you remember learning how to walk? Chances are you don't. But it's a pretty good bet that you received a lot of positive reinforcement during the process. The process of teaching a young child to walk for the first time is one that can be followed in many other areas of a child's development.

What if we stood a small child on his wobbly feet and said, "walk," and then when he fell down we spanked him for not walking. Sound ridiculous? Of course. A child spanked for falling down will not try to walk since he knows this leads to punishment. Therefore, parents should first help a child learn how to stand up. If he stands for even a second or two, they hug and kiss him and shower him with praise. The first halting steps bring even more excitement and encouragement. The slightest progress is rewarded. Buoyed by the prospect of reward, the child keeps trying, until the desired behavior (in this case, walking) is achieved.

Praising children for making progress is easy. It's a simple matter of seeing progress and immediately letting the child know you're pleased with what you see. It's also appropriate to tell the child how you feel about the progress and explain why the improvement is appreciated by the parent or the family as a whole. You can take the opportunity to encourage children to keep up the good work and add some physical contact, like a kiss, pat on the back or a hug.

The type of reinforcement used depends on the individual child. For example, seven-year old Andrew, who has trouble keeping his room clean, has been begging his parents for a new bicycle. His parents might use the bicycle as positive reinforcement to get Andrew to clean up his room, telling him that if his room starts looking better, he might expect to find the bike he wants under the Christmas tree.

Assuming that Andrew is able but unwilling to keep his room clean, the promise of the bicycle may provide the incentive he needs. Samantha, who also dislikes cleaning up her room, may have no interest whatsoever in a new bike. She may be interested instead in having some of her friends over for a slumber party. Thus, her parents may use a different reinforcer to produce the same result as Andrew's parents.

At this point you may be asking, "Isn't this really a not-so-subtle form of bribery?" Some parents may be concerned about their children becoming dependent on rewards for everything they do and worried that they are locking themselves into a system where the child's only incentive to good behavior is personal gain. Observation has shown that this is not the case. Children who are reinforced early for Positive Behavior and then gradually allowed to assume more responsibility on their own usually become happy, self-motivated children who can be left on their own without risk of consequences. In other words, it appears to work.

Don't Reinforce Unwanted Behavior

Problems can result when parents pay attention to their children only when they are behaving poorly. Andrew and his sister Carol fight most of the time even though their parents punish them when they do. When asked what they do when the children come home from school and behave well, the parents reply, "We don't do anything. We expect good behavior."

When their parents have guests, it is not unusual for a scene like the following to occur. When Andrew attempts to get his father's attention (even when he is behaving properly), his father says, "Andrew, don't interrupt. The adults are talking."

After several futile attempts to get his parents' attention, Andrew goes over and punches Carol on the arm. Immediately he has the attention of both his parents. Andrew soon learns that if he wants his parents' attention, which is rewarding to him, all he has to do is misbehave. In fact, he is willing to endure his parents' punishment in order to get their attention. In the long run Andrew's parents are reinforcing the very behavior they do not want, and discouraging the appropriate behavior they do want.

Parents will sometimes use short-term remedies for immediate situations, without thinking of the long-term consequences. A crying child is given a piece of candy, and stops crying. But from this the child learns to cry whenever it wants candy. This is an example of a parenting effort that is successful in accomplishing an immediate result, but totally ineffective, and in fact counter-effective, in the long run.

How Situational Parenting Grows Winners

The key elements in the parenting strategy of "growing winners" are risk-taking and positive reinforcement. The following illustration shows how these two important concepts fit into the Situational Parenting® Model.

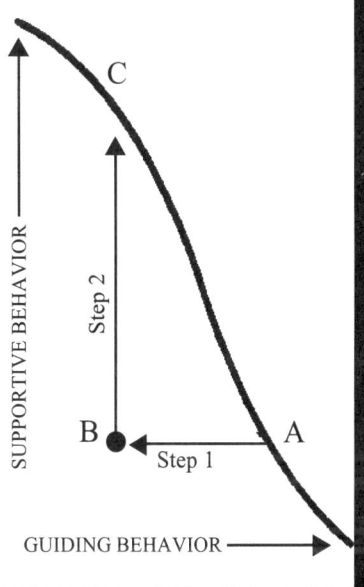

DEVELOPMENTAL CYCLE

There are two important steps you take to develop a child's readiness:

Step 1. Gradually reduce the amount of Guiding Behavior you use.

- Take calculated risks
- Use small steps
- Don't punish

Step 2. If the child responds well, use Supportive Behavior as a reinforcement.

- For children at levels R1 and R2 reinforce by slightly increasing SUPPORTIVE Behavior
- For children at levels R3 and R4 reinforce by slightly decreasing SUPPORTIVE Behavior.

If a parent wants to develop a child's readiness in a certain area where the child is low in readiness, the first step is to provide guidance (Step A). This is the R1-S1 style matching we discussed earlier. If the child makes decent progress, the next thing the parent should do is reduce the amount of guidance (Step B). This involves taking a risk, since the child has not yet performed this task without the parent's close supervision. If the child succeeds, the parent responds with positive reinforcement that represents an increase in Supportive Behavior (Step C). The end result is that parent and child have each moved progressively along the bell curve.

This strategy can work anywhere along the development path, whatever the child's level of readiness may be. For example, in moving from S3 to S4, the parent should reinforce the child by providing less support, since a child in that situation will regard the parents' hands-off approach as evidence of earned trust.

The Stages of Development

The following illustration shows us the sequence of Parenting Styles to be used as the child develops readiness in a particular area. When a child is low in readiness (R1), the parent needs to use S1, providing the necessary guidance the child needs to comply with the task satisfactorily. This approach is called **guiding**. As the child moves to R2, the parent needs to provide a reduced, but still high, level of guidance, but needs to combine this with a high level of support. S2 on the development cycle is called **explaining**. The **guiding** (or S1) approach has served its purpose; the parent must now add support as well as guidance.

DEVELOPMENTAL CYCLE

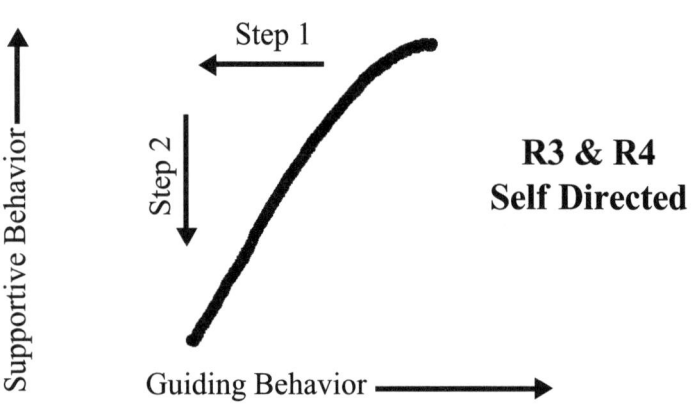

As the child's level of readiness moves beyond the Model's midpoint, the parent begins to withdraw guidance allowing the child to make more decisions on his own. His ability is growing. He now needs encouragement rather than instruction. Consequently, S3 is characterized by **encouraging**. Finally, as the child moves into the highest level of readiness, the parent reduces the amount of Supportive Behavior as well, until he is simply **observing** the child's behavior and providing occassional reinforcement.

Guiding, explaining, encouraging, observing. These are the steps needed to grow winners. However, the Situational Parenting® Model is merely a blueprint. Only with dedicated effort on your part will it become a structurally sound building.

Of course, it would be a wonderfully predictable world if all children moved steadily upward in terms of readiness and never slipped backwards. In the next chapter we're going to discuss how you can recognize slippage in your child's behavior and do something constructive about it.

You cannot shout away hurt,
Nor can you heal in silence,
The heart must whisper its cure.

Chapter Six
Discipline -vs- Punishment
(or Stopping Slippage)

It would be great if parents only had to respond to increased levels of readiness in their children. But, as any parent knows, this is not the case. For one reason or another, children often begin to exhibit less responsibility in a given area than they had before. In short, they regress or slip.

Dana's parents both work full-time, and because their time is limited, they expect a lot of help around the house from Dana and her two younger brothers. Dana has always shown an interest in cooking. An interest her busy mother encourages. By the time she was fifteen, Dana was preparing two evening meals a week for the family, which not only took a load off her overworked mother, but stimulated Dana's culinary creativity as well.

Of course, some meals were more successful than others and her two brothers could be counted on to provide pointed criticism whenever failures occurred. But Dana enjoyed cooking for the family and her parents appreciated her efforts. Then Dana found a steady boyfriend and everything changed. She began missing her turn in the cooking rotation or throwing something together at the last minute.

When gently reminded by her parents, she would protest that she did not have time. Finally, she told her parents that she wasn't interested in cooking for the family any more.

Dana's level of readiness for the task of cooking had changed. She had slipped from being "able, willing and confident" (R4) to being "able but unwilling" (R3). Her parents, who had encouraged her along the curve to the highest level of readiness, now faced the prospect of seeing everyone's efforts come undone.

Here's a different example of slippage. Eleven year old Ethan is eager to learn how to play baseball and today his dad decides to take him into the yard for a practice session. They throw the ball back and forth, slowly at first, then Dad puts a little more "zip" on the ball.

One of Dad's throws comes in too fast, goes through Ethan's outstretched hands and lands squarely on the child's nose. Dad rushes over to wipe away the tears. After a few moments, Ethan's distress is reduced to sniffles. He looks up and says, "I don't think I want to learn this game!"

Ethan and Dana are both going through what the Situational Parenting® Model terms slippage — a decrease in the level of readiness. As with the developmental cycle described in the preceding chapter, there are ways for parents to deal with this slippage. The specific strategies differ, but the goal is the same — instilling in your children a sense of responsibility that encompasses both ability and motivation.

The Regressive Cycle

One of the most difficult tasks a parent faces is arresting regressive behavior. Parents often tend to be so concerned about developing responsibility and independence in their children that they don't know what to do once they've made that effort, seen it succeed and then watched the child slip backwards. They are often victims of their own raised expectations, failing to realize that any learning experience is uneven and that backsliding will usually be part of the process.

Adjusting Parenting Style

Situational Parents realize that when performance slips, they need to adapt their style according to the new readiness levels of their children. They don't ignore performance problems, but take responsibility for intervening and turning things around. Making a timely intervention and adjusting Parenting Styles is essential in the regressive cycle.

Dana used to be at the highest level of readiness for sharing in the family cooking duties. She was able and willing to do her share, and thus her parents used S4 (low support and low guidance), letting her take most of the responsibility for getting the job done. But now she is no longer willing to help. She has slipped from R4 to R3, and her parents must make an intervention in the corresponding area. The previous use of delegating or monitoring is replaced with problem solving, listening and depending on Dana. Something has happened for (or to) Dana to cause this regression. If Dana slips further, her parents' Parenting Style must also regress from encouraging, through S2 all the way back to S1, if necessary.

Constructive Discipline

Many people tend to interpret discipline as punishment. It's the problem-solving nature of constructive discipline that differentiates it from punishment. We're not saying that kids never need punishment. Children need to be aware that there are consequences for any action and unwanted behavior can evoke punishment from their parents and other authority figures.

Constructive discipline is designed to be a learning process that provides an opportunity for positive growth. Parents need to recognize that when performance slips, they need to adapt their style accordingly. Even when an *observing style* is appropriate, they monitor results so they're aware if changes in performance occur.

Treat Children Where They Are

When a child's performance slips, the intervention must be made with a Parenting Style that is appropriate for the child's current level of readiness. A common trap parents fall into is to see the slippage, but because of previous higher readiness levels, take the "wait and see" approach. Conversely, there is also the trap of over reacting in our style change. We see a bit of slippage and intervene with all the drama and energy of correcting this grievous act only to find out it was nothing. Children need to be treated according to the manner in which they are presently performing, regardless of previously demonstrated readiness and discounting performance potential.

Timeliness

Problem solving must be done in a timely manner. The sooner the intervention takes place, the better the chance of stopping the performance slippage. The longer you wait, the more directive your intervention will have to be, in which case you'll risk your child becoming anxious, frustrated or resentful. Even when the directive intervention is appropriate, it may lead to the child's attempts to get out from under the parents.

For example, you expect your children to keep their rooms clean. Over the past few months they have done a good job of keeping their rooms in shape. Lately, however, when you walk by one child's room, it's a mess. You begin to complain to each other about the child's lack of performance, but you don't mention it to your child.

Finally, one day you've had it. The room is a disaster and you can't wait for your child to get home so you can really let him have it. Your child feels "zapped." He's bitter toward you, and he doesn't focus on the importance of keeping the room clean.

If you had intervened earlier, an Encouraging Style might have been enough to turn the problem around. But now, the highly structured style is necessary and creates resentment in the child. This is a trap that parents often fall into when making disciplinary interventions. First, they engage in ostrich parenting by avoiding the issues and hoping the problem will go away. Then when it doesn't, they get angry and "zap" the child. This all too common pattern (S4 to S1) is what we refer to as the "leave 'em alone, zap 'em syndrome."

By timing interventions appropriately and treating children where they are currently performing, parents can begin to take a proactive approach to problem solving as opposed to just reacting to each new crisis.

Is it ever appropriate to make a quick change backward in style? The answer is a qualified yes. For example, Bobby, who has always done well in math, is suddenly close to failing with only three weeks to go in the grading period. His teacher informs his parents that he has handed in only two out of seven homework assignments. Their S4 approach has obviously not been working. Bobby's level of readiness has slipped dramatically, to R2 or perhaps even R1.

Bobby's parents need to determine first whether he's simply having trouble with new concepts or if he has lost his motivation to work, or both. If Bobby indicates that he does not care about his poor performance and will not do his homework, then the parents need to shift directly to S1 to deal with this drastic change in readiness.

Chances are, if the parents had been informed earlier of Bobby's problem, they might have intervened at a higher level of readiness. If Bobby's performance indicates that he has lost ability too, they'll have to adjust their Parenting Style all the way back to S1, and tell him exactly what to do, how, when and where to do it. They will need to maximize their involvement in homework assignments and studying until Bobby's back on track.

Varying The Emotional Level

The emotional level of the intervention is different for constructive discipline than for developing children's levels of readiness. When developing readiness, you're attempting to expand the current ability of the child. Therefore, it helps to keep the emotional temperature of a developmental intervention at a low level.

People often misinterpret Situational Parenting® because they think guiding or directing means raising their voice or yelling. Actually, an S1 approach can be a very soft and caring approach, by providing needed demonstration of how to do things with "hands on" guidance. It would be inappropriate to shout or raise the emotional level with children who are developing. It could make them insecure about taking risks and continuing to learn in the future.

However, when children choose not to use their current ability, and constructive discipline is appropriate, you might raise the emotional level one or two decibels. This helps to get the children's attention and lets them know that you're not only aware of the performance problem, but that you care about the solution.

Focus on Performance

The next thing to consider in working with constructive discipline is not to attack personality. Focus on the child's performance rather than the child himself. We need to remember that there's no change in terms of caring for the child. It's the behavior that's not acceptable. We can't accomplish much if we attack the child's self-worth.

As parents, we have an obligation to protect and build the child's sense of self. Children get profound messages regarding what they really mean to us in the difficult moments and not just when things are going well. When slippage occurs it becomes a moment of truth ... "Are you mad at me?" ... "Do you hate me?" ... "Am I going to get away with this?" There is simply no appropriate place for character assassination.

In a moment of anger a parent might say something like, "I just told you that a week ago. Can't you remember anything, you idiot?" These attacks on personality make children angry and the probability of working successfully with them is much lower than when parents focus specifically on the behavior that is unacceptable. All we really accomplish is to raise the emotional level of our children, but we don't get them to focus on the problem. When the focus is on performance rather than personality, both parent and child can talk about the problem and solve it together.

Be Specific ... Do Your Homework

Constructive discipline requires specific statements. It's difficult for children to know what they're doing wrong if parents communicate with them in generalities.

So often parents accomplish all other aspects of constructive discipline well. They treat children where they are... they make timely interventions ... they keep a moderate emotional profile... and they focus directly on performance. However, they often sound like this, "Look, you're just not behaving like I know you can. Now get with it." That leaves children bewildered or angry, because they just don't understand what's expected of them.

Generalities don't get the job done. Parents have to do their homework before making interventions. They should gather specific information to use in describing the problem and suggesting a solution. Being specific means saying things like, "You didn't call me before ten o'clock last night, so I didn't know what time you'd be home." Or, "You started to clean your room, but you left your underwear on the bed and your socks on the floor." Or, "I asked you yesterday not to hit your brother, and now you pinched his arm." That's how parents should talk specifically with their children, so that both parties can work together toward a solution.

Keep It Private

Effective Parents remember to keep disciplinary interventions private. As a guideline, it's a good idea to praise children in public and criticize in private. If parents jump on their children when others are around, they risk making them more concerned about getting yelled at in front of others than identifying what's wrong and solving the problem. Discussing problems in private tends to make it easier to get your point across and keep children focused on the problem-solving process. Plus, the extra minute needed to secure privacy is wisely used to gain your composure and gather your thoughts.

Constructive discipline should make problem-solving a positive growth opportunity instead of a punitive experience. It's important to:
- **Treat** children where they are currently performing
- **Make** the intervention immediately
- **Use** appropriate emotional levels
- **Focus** on performance
- **Be specific**
- **Keep** the intervention private

The Situational Parenting® Model

Earlier we discussed the relationship of the developmental cycle to the four levels of readiness and the corresponding Parenting Styles. We referred to Style 1 as **guiding**; Style 2 as **explaining**; Style 3 as **encouraging**, and the fourth style and final level (when the child has assumed nearly full responsibility for his behavior/performance), as **observing**.

Obviously, in the regressive cycle, we cannot simply proceed as if the child had never attained the higher level of Readiness from which he has now slipped. For one thing, our expectations have changed. We are no longer trying to help our child reach goals he has never attained before; rather, we are attempting to halt the child's slippage and get him back on the upward track. Acknowledgement of the child's earlier progress and his ability to return to that level is inherent in our strategy for stopping slippage.

REGRESSIVE CYCLE

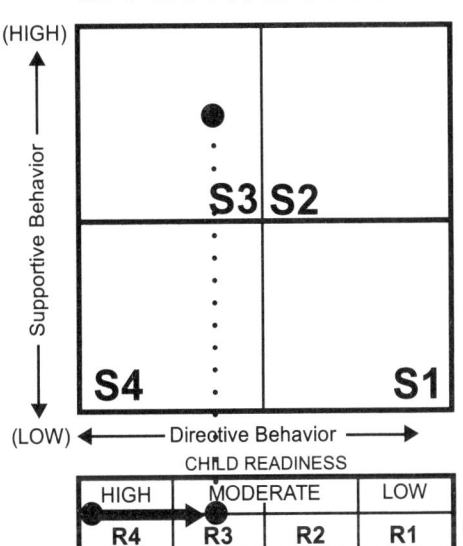

Reminders:

- Make the intervention timely
- Use an appropriate emotional level
- Focus on performance, not personality
- Be specific ... do your homework
- Keep the intervention private
- Respond to children where they are presently performing

When a child begins to slip, but is still at R4, our first task as parents is to **monitor** the child's behavior, to determine where and when an intervention might be necessary. If the child slips back into R3, becoming unwilling to perform a task previously done without complaint, or losing confidence for some reason, we should then switch to a **problem solving** approach. This may involve sitting down with the child and helping him to define the problem. Discussion should focus on the child's ability to solve the problem himself. As the Model indicates, we have raised our level of support, while still leaving much of the guidance in the child's hands.

Further slippage, into R2, calls for **persuading**. Now the child has slipped to a point where more guidance is needed. Persuasion can take many forms. We saw an example of one type earlier in this chapter with Dana and the cooking duties. Another case might be that of a child who has mastered a task, only to forget several days later how to do it. In this case, a gentle reminder accompanied by a few instructions may be all that is needed.

If a child slips backwards into R1, the lowest level of readiness, we need to **direct** that child's behavior. This differs from the up-the-scale task of **guiding**, in that the child has already been shown what to do, how to do it and has done it in the past. He must simply be told to do it now.

It's important to note that slippage can occur anywhere along the scale. Few slippages in fact, are so dramatic and irreversible that the parents must slide their style all the way from S4 to S1. Learning, as we have said before, is not something one accomplishes all at once. A child who has just achieved R2 in a certain area can easily slide back into R1 if the proper support and guidance are not maintained. Likewise, a child who has reached R3 can slip back to R2, put himself back on track with your help, reach R4 and slide back to R3, where he will need a different type of help than before.

If we as parents keep abreast of our children and how they are doing in the areas of their lives we want to influence, we can catch slippage soon after it starts and keep it to a minimum. In this context, constructive discipline and problem solving become helpful tools in the parent-child relationship.

Stray from the text for a few moments and try to imagine yourself backpacking on a wilderness trail. Part of your goal for this outing is to collect a number of fist-sized rocks. You are being selective and in doing so you have covered a considerable distance. The hike has been a great success and your backpack is full of the perfect rocks. On your return you are on a downhill trail with several steep declines and gullies. You come to the first steep gully and thinking about the angle of the path and the awkward weight on your back you are aware that you need to be careful. With the best of intentions and fore thought you start down the steep embankment. You have underestimated the impact that the weight in your backpack will have on your balance and your ability to stop. With each step of your decent you are uncontrollably gaining momentum. There is no stopping, no control and you careen off the cliff side and grab onto a tree trying your best to prolong the inevitable crash. And it does.

Let this story represent your parenting day. We begin by expecting and even hoping for the best. Go into the kitchen and the last of the milk is sitting on the counter from the night before. Jimmy has been told to put the milk back in the refrigerator at least a dozen times. You have just picked up an emotional rock and put it into your backpack.

Leaving the kitchen you continue your hike into the family room hoping to catch a couple minutes of the morning news before taking off to work. You are not looking for it but there it is, an open bag of chips all over the table and the floor. Two empty dirty glasses, assorted dirty clothes thrown about and a few school books scattered on the floor. You have another emotional rock for your backpack.

Saying nothing you leave for work only to open the front door and step on the skateboard – another rock. While at work you get a call from the school, they are a little upset that you have not responded to the three letters they have sent regarding lost library book fees and Jimmy will not get his report card until the fees are paid – another rock.

Upon arriving home you walk in to hear the television playing a bit loud, something that really irritates you – another rock. You walk into the family room where the television is blaring and Jimmy isn't there – another rock.

The backpack is now so full of emotional rocks you can't zip the darn thing up. Just than Jimmy walks into the room sporting a large grape juice stain on the brand new $49.00 designer sport shirt he just had to have. Your eyes roll and everything becomes a blur and you are not even fully aware of the words coming from your mouth. With all the weight of the overfilled backpack you just can't stop!

It is as complicated and as simple as this: you know when you have been collecting rocks. Acknowledge it. The extra weight will throw your control off. There really is no choice if you are going to be in control of what and how you talk to Jimmy. You need to empty that backpack. Yes, even in a regressive intervention it is important to articulate and show care, concern, empathy and love.

From the parent to the child…
My life would be so simple
If I only needed to be your friend
That would be easy
But I have a greater responsibility
To love you to guide you
I am your parent.

Chapter Seven
Because I said so…

When all the reasons and explanations have proven to be of little or no avail. The books and advice on child rearing don't seem to address the issue at hand. All your instincts are screaming at you to listen. And your child's reasoning is sounding more convincing, yet you know "it" isn't right. There is a bottom line… "Because I said so."

Parenting is a richly rewarding job that is twenty four hours a day, seven days a week. It isn't a one hour counseling session every other week without everyday life intervening between sessions. Parenting doesn't afford us that objectivity, professional therapy background or communications skills. Sometimes we have nothing left but our hearts and our instincts.

It is in those moments that the most honest answer we have to offer is "Because I said so."

"Because I said so" should always be held in a special reserve position. Simply put, if it is overused the respect of the parent's right to invoke such a statement is diminished. Overuse reduces acceptance and effectiveness. Under use presents its own set of problems. First, when there is reluctance on the parent's part to simply *call the shots* and yet the conversation is awkwardly continuing with no closure in sight, you've won nothing. When the parent fails to make their point, it appears that talking was a waste of time, particularly to the child. The longer the child presents their reasoning the more the parent sounds unreasonable. At a minimum ask yourself, why create the confusion that an issue is negotiable when your mind is already made up?

As we close the chapter on this book we'd like to remind you that Situational Parenting® doesn't end when you close this book. It is a life long commitment full of ups and downs, joys and sorrows, success and effectiveness. If we truly want to do the best that we can, we have to remind ourselves that mistakes will be made, lessons will be learned and behavioral modeling will be achieved. We invite you to read "A Child's Ten Commandments for Parents." Just like Dorothy Nolte's poem, "Children Learn What They Live," this piece seeks to remind you that your children won't be the same age forever and it is important to take the time to not only watch them grow and develop, but help them get there.

A Child's Ten Commandments for Parents.

1. My hands are small; please don't expect perfection whenever I make my bed, draw a picture or throw a ball. My legs are short. Please slow down so that I can keep up with you.

2. My eyes have not seen the world as yours have, please let me explore safely. Don't restrict me unnecessarily.

3. Housework will always be there. I'm only little for such a short time-please take the time to explain things to me about this wonderful world and do so willingly.

4. My feelings are tender; please be sensitive to my needs; don't nag me all day long. (You wouldn't want to be nagged for your inquisitiveness). Treat me, as you would like to be treated.

5. I'm a special gift; please treasure me as my Creator intended you to do, holding me accountable for my actions, giving me guidelines to live by and disciplining me in a loving manner.

6. I need your encouragement, not just your praise to grow. Please go easy on the criticism; you can criticize the things I do without criticizing me.

7. Please give me the freedom to make decisions concerning myself. Permit me to fail, so that I can learn from my own mistakes. Then someday I will be prepared to make the kind of decisions life will require of me.

8. Please don't do things over for me. Somehow that makes me feel that my efforts didn't quite measure up to your expectations. I know it's hard, but please don't try to compare me to my brother or sister.

9. Please don't be afraid to leave for a weekend together. Kids need a vacation from parents, just as parents need a vacation from kids. Besides it's a great way to show us kids that your marriage is very special.

10. Please set a good example for me to follow in all the ways of life. I enjoy watching the things you do and want to do them just like you do.

- *Author Unknown*

INDEX

A Child's Ten Commandments for Parents	105
Ability	32
Ability and Willingness	30-33
Able and Unwilling or Able but Insecure	48-49
Able and Willing and Confident	42, 50
Able but Insecure	40,48-49
Able but Unwilling	40,48-49
Acceptance	74-75
Andrew (S1)	15-17,29-31,79-82
Apathy	9
Attitude vs. Behavior	55
Because I said so	103-104
Ben (S4)	25
Bobby (R4-R2)	33,92
Brandy (R1)	30,36
Carol (Behavior Reinforcement)	81-82
Carrie and Bill (S4)	25
Center for Leadership Studies	7
Character Assassination	94
Children Learn What They Live	12
Chris (S1)	22
Connie (R3)	40
Constructive Discipline	88,90,92,94
Dana (R4-R3)	87-79,96,98
Decision-making	23,73
Demonstrating or Demonstrated	8,32-33
Develop	34
Development (Stages)	84
Development(al) Cycle	83-84,96
Diagnose	60
Direct	98
Direct Guidance	73
Directive Behavior	18-19,21-22,57,61
Dynamic(s)	33-34,77
Effective Parenting or Parents	9,20,95
Effective Styles	97
Effectiveness	8,59
Emotional Level	93
Encouraging	24,85,96

Ethan (R2-R1) 88
Examples
  Andrew (S1) 15-17,29-31,79-82
  Ben (S4) 25
  Bobby (R4-R2) 33,99
  Brandy (R1) 30,36
  Carol (Behavior Reinforcement) 81-82gh
  Carrie and Bill (S4) 25
  Chris (S1) 22
  Connie (R3) 40
  Dana (R4-R3) 87-89,98
  Ethan (R2-R1) 88
  Gerry (S2) 56
  Jason (R3) 40
  Jimmy (Emotional Rocks) 99,100
  Johnny (S3) 24
  Marcos (R2 – Skamp) 38
  Mark (R3) 67-69
  Marty ((R1) 62,63
  Mike (S2) 23
  Pat (R2) 38
  Pat (R4) 71,72
  Pete (S1) 22
  Randy (R4 – Taco King) 42
  Sally (S4) 16-18,29
  Sanchez teenagers (S3) 24
  Sarah (R2) 64-65
  Skamp (R2 – Marcos) 38
  Stephanie (S2) 23
  Taco King (R4 – Randy) 42
  Terry (R1) 36
  Timmy (R3) 40
  Tom (S2) 56
  Tony (S4) 56
Explaining 84,96
Generalities 94,95
Gerry (S2) 56
Goal setting 78
Guidance 17-18,73,98
Guidance and Support 17-18,73
Guiding 21,84-85,98
Guiding Behavior 83

How do we show it?	10-11
Individual Dynamic	31
Influence	8
Jason (R3)	40
Jimmy (Emotional Rocks)	99-100
Johnny (S3)	24
Keep it Private	95
Leadership training	30
Leave 'em alone, zap 'em syndrome	91
Marcos (R2 – Skamp)	38
Mark (R3)	67-69
Marty (R1)	62-63
Matching Process (The)	61
Mike (S2)	23
Misdiagnosed	33
Monitor	97
Nolte, Dorothy	11-12,104
Observer	73
Observing	85,96
Observing Style	90
Ostrich parenting	91
Parent(ing) Behavior	17-21,57,59-65,70
Parenting Style(s)	55-57,59,72,84
Pat (R2)	38
Pat (R4)	71-72
Performance	93
Persuading	98
Pete (S1)	22
Positive Behavior	81
Positive Reinforcement	79
Problem Solving	97
Randy (R4 – Taco KinG)	42
Reactive	15
Readiness	30,44,52,56
Child	31,34,37,39-41,43,58-59
Cue Library	44
Cues	48
Dynamic	34
Factors	35
Level(s)	51-52,58,60,74
Level 1 or R1	37,44-45,62,98
Brandy	30,36

Marty	62-63
Terry	36
Level 2 or R2	39,46-47,63,98
Ethan	88
Marcos	38
Pat	38
Sarah	64-65
Level 3 or R3	41,48-49,64-67,89,98
Connie	40
Jason	40
Mark	67-69
Timmy	40
Level 4 or R4	43,50-51,70-71,75,98
Bobby	33,92
Dana	87-89,98
Pat	71,72
Randy	42
Ready	30
Ready, Willing and Able	58
Recognition	10
Positive	10
Negative	10
Conditional	10
Extinction	10
Regress(ion)	34
Regressive Cycle (The)	89,96,97
Sally (S4)	16-18,29
Sanchez teenagers (S3)	24
Sarah (R2)	64-65
Self Directed	84
Situational Parent(s) or Parenting	88,93,96,104
Skamp (R2 – Marcos)	38
Slippage	85,87-91,94,98
Specific Task	59
Stephanie (S2)	23
Stroking	17

Style(s)	26
Style 1 or S1	22,62-63,73-74,93,96,98
Andrew	15-17
Chris	22
Pete	22,74
Style 2 or S2	23,64-65,73,75,96
Gerry	56
Mike	23
Stephanie	23
Tom	56
Style 3 or S3	24,66-67-69,73,75,96,
Johnny	24
Sanchez teenagers	24
Style 4 or S4	25,70-71,73,75,96,98
Ben	25
Carrie and Bill	25
Sally	16-18,29
Tony	56
Success	8,59
Support	17-18
Supporting or Supportive Behavior	8-19,21,22,25,57,61,83
Taco King (R4 – Randy)	42
Task specific	30
Terry (R1)	36
Timmy (R3)	40
Tom (S2)	56
Tony (S4)	56
Two-way communication	23
Unable and Insecure	36
Unable and Unwilling	36
Unable and Unwilling and Unable and Insecure	44-45
Unable and Willing or Confident	46-47
Unable but Confident	38
Unable but Willing	38
Unmotivated or Unwilling	33
Value Sets	55
Why don't we show it?	11
Willingness	32
Willingness-Unwillingness	33
Zapped	91

For information on Situational Leadership, Sales Service and Team training programs, instrumentation and related materials contact:

Center for Leadership Studies
230 West Third Avenue
Escondido, CA 92025-4180
(760) 741-6595

Visit our web at :
www.situational.com
or
www.situationalparenting.com